M000279412

ICONS

The Essential Collection

SR. FAITH RICCIO, CJ

FOREWORD BY
FREDERICA MATHEWES-GREEN

PARACLETE PRESS
BREWSTER, MASSACHUSETTS

2016 First and Second Printing

Icons: The Essential Collection

Copyright © 2016 by The Community of Jesus, Inc.

ISBN 978-1-61261-831-9

Scripture quotations marked NRSV are from New Revised Standard Version Bible, copyright © 1989 National Council of the Churches of Christ in the United States of America. Used by permission. All rights reserved.

Scripture quotations marked NIV are taken from THE HOLY BIBLE, NEW INTERNATIONAL VERSION® NIV® Copyright © 1973, 1978, 1984 by International Bible Society®. Used by permission. All rights reserved worldwide.

Scripture quotations marked KJV are taken from the King James Version of the Holy Bible.

The Paraclete Press name and logo (dove on cross) are trademarks of Paraclete Press, Inc.

Library of Congress Cataloging-in-Publication Data

Names: Riccio, Faith, author.
Title: Icons : the essential collection / Sr. Faith Riccio, CJ ; foreword by
    Frederica Mathewes-Green.
Description: Brewster MA : Paraclete Press Inc., 2016. | Includes
    bibliographical references.
Identifiers: LCCN 2016021924 | ISBN 9781612618319 (hard cover)
Subjects: LCSH: Christian art and symbolism. | Theology. | Icons.
Classification: LCC BV150 .R45 2016 | DDC 246/.53--dc23
LC record available at https://lccn.loc.gov/2016021924

10 9 8 7 6 5 4 3 2

All rights reserved. No portion of this book may be reproduced, stored in an electronic retrieval system, or transmitted in any form or by any means—electronic, mechanical, photocopy, recording, or any other—except for brief quotations in printed reviews, without the prior permission of the publisher.

Published by Paraclete Press
Brewster, Massachusetts
www.paracletepress.com
Printed in the United States of America

Contents

Foreword

THE FIRST THING WE EVER SEE IS A FACE.

The first thing a newborn's eyes seek out is another pair of eyes. When an infant finds its mother's or father's eyes, it locks into them, and that mutual gaze forges a connection to last a lifetime. Researchers have found that, when a newborn is shown a series of simple line drawings, it will always prefer to look at a simple oval with two dots near the top—the simplest depiction of a human face. A newborn will do this, even though it has never seen a face before.

God created us with a desire to seek out faces, to look *into* faces, for that is where we read the complex mystery of human life: the mystery of personhood. This is a genuine need, and those who are deprived of other's faces, as in solitary confinement, suffer profoundly. Without one another's faces, we don't know who we are.

Our Lord chose to put on a face, to become visible in a form we find familiar, because we already know how to love another person. When we look at the faces in these icons, whether of our Lord or of his friends, we meet with vi ⌁ I C O N S

something we already know, for by now we have seen many, many faces. We know how the image of a loved one connects us to her, in some inexpressible way. We understand that we can look at and handle such a photo tenderly, with love, without thinking that the photo *is* the person. We honor, but do not worship, icons.

The Greek word "icon" (*eikon)* appears throughout the Scriptures, beginning with Genesis 1:26—God made us in his "*eikon* and likeness." Christ, too, is the "the *eikon* of the invisible God" (Col. 1:15). When God designed the human form at the beginning of Creation, it was with the future Incarnation in mind; it was with the foreknowledge that Christ would one day put on a form and a face like ours.

The images in this book will present to us, over and over, that mystery of personhood, as we encounter the face of Christ and of those who loved him. In looking at the icons in this book, we can remember who we are, and what we are called to be, as we are continuously being "conformed to the *eikon* of his Son" (Rom. 8:29).

—FREDERICA MATHEWES-GREEN

Introduction

ICONS ARE AN INVITATION TO GO BEYOND OUR WORLD and to take a moment to look as through a window into heaven. But they are more than just a place for observation. The space they create gives us a wonderful, loving, and open access to reach out toward God and know him deeply in a new way. They are meant to enrich our spiritual lives and generate a conversation with God. They were created to touch and form us; they have a tangible ability to soothe and confront where necessary. Icons ask us to spend time with them, to get to know the saint, the scene, the illumined moment in the spiritual dimension that we can eventually draw strength from and live with.

I have been asked many times how to "read" an icon, how to interpret its symbolism, how to understand it. Over the years my answer has increasingly been that each icon is expressing a person or moment that we need to live with to know. Icons require only that we spend time conversing with them. They are in the truest sense a place to gather our wandering attention and direct it toward God. I think God knows an icon can keep our attention and focus our desire.

In our church we have a small prayer chapel that contains a shelf on which rest icons portraying twelve saints who stand and watch with us, granting us graceful moments in a heavenly space. They create a friendly quiet place of acceptance, and the feeling of support and encouragement from the saints permeates the atmosphere as we allow the silence to slowly envelop us. Whether we are in turmoil, saddened by a loss, or hopeful for the day ahead, many of us come to light a candle in front of one of the icons and spend time praying with the saints the icons portray. They are always ready to hear, to love, to capture our attention, and to direct us toward God. They join with us and comfort us and point us toward the place where our heart finds Christ and rests in him.

Icons reveal the essence of the subject's relationship with God; they touch that space where God meets earth in a needy human being. So they come to us as they may look in heaven, offering a helping hand and showing us how to just sit with Jesus and pour out all our concerns, fears, and anxieties until we can stand again, hopeful and resolved to move forward. The time spent just praying with them forms us, changes us. There are times I have felt carried by them and times I have felt confronted by the saints' courage, by their "yes" to God, and above by all their individual relationship with Jesus.

Icons express spiritual reality. Though they are stylized we can feel the form and life force beneath the painting.

They are a part of a spiritual legacy that has the strength of the ages behind it. Opening oneself to this legacy joins one to the movement of God's world. It is like participating in the powerful flow of God's love all about us as he endeavors to draw us to himself much as a river will pick up and carry a floating branch.

Icons challenge our busyness and give us a place to simply unwind. Often we do not want to calm down; we like the hype of living, or we are in a situation where we are in constant movement and worry. The icon gently gives us an opportunity to rest and begin to heal.

The most difficult thing is to continue to quiet ourselves and allow the Holy Spirit to touch us. There is a feeling of vulnerability and helplessness that we must embrace as the relationship grows. This is difficult. And yet the icon in its straightforward simplicity and strength reminds us that God carries us more than we struggle to remain in his presence. The icon states that he is there for us; we need just lean in and stay with him. That alone is enough. We may feel bewildered and helpless; we may not have the appropriate feelings of prayer; but there we can focus and give our time and thoughtfulness to God. The right feelings are not required—just attention and care given to finding him.

The Icons

THE PANTOCRATOR

[Jesus] emptied himself,
  taking the form of a slave,
  being born in human likeness.
And being found in human form,
he humbled himself
  and became obedient to the point of death—
  even death on a cross.
Therefore God also highly exalted him
  and gave him the name
  that is above every name

—PHILIPPIANS 2:7–11 NRSV

THE PANTOCRATOR

Remember, you are held safe.
You are loved.
You are protected.

You are in communion with God and with those whom God has sent you. What is of God will last. It belongs to the eternal life. Choose it, and it will be yours.

—HENRI J. M. NOUWEN

PANTOCRATOR

The word *Pantocrator* is of Greek origin and means "ruler of all." The full-faced icon holds the book of the Gospels in his left hand and blesses us with his right hand. The icon portrays Christ as the Righteous Judge and the Lover of Mankind. The Gospel is the book by which we are judged, and the blessing proclaims God's loving kindness toward us, showing us that he is granting us his forgiveness.

THE PANTOCRATOR, detail

 ANTHONY

Therefore, my dear brothers and sisters,
stand firm. Let nothing move you.
Always give yourselves fully
to the work of the Lord,
because you know that
your labor in the Lord is not in vain.

—1 CORINTHIANS 15:58 NIV

ANTHONY

One day in church Anthony heard Matthew 19:21:

If you wish to be perfect, go, sell your possessions, and give the money to the poor, and you will have treasure in heaven; then come, follow me.

Eventually he went outside the village to live a life of praying, fasting, and manual labor. He always told those who came to visit him that the key to the ascetic life is perseverance. Many people came to seek Anthony. Gradually a number of disciples established themselves in caves and in huts around him. Thus was formed a colony of ascetics who begged him to come and be their guide in the spiritual life—which he did.

ANTHONY 251–356

Though there were other hermits in his time, Anthony of Egypt is sometimes called the "father of monasticism" because of his early dedication to a balanced life of solitude, asceticism, and prayer. Reading an account of his life is part of what inspired Augustine's conversion to Christianity a generation later.

ANTHONY, detail

 # BENEDICT

Never lose hope
in the mercy of God.

—BENEDICT

BENEDICT

Benedict is saying,

> *"Wake up!*
> *Open your eyes!*
> *Open your ears!*
> *Let the divine life and light*
> *invade you so that your life is filled*
> *with aspiration, joy and hope."*

There is a God who so loves you and wants to give you everything, including himself. God wants to bring you into fullness of divine joy and life. That is what it is all about. When we are in touch with that, there is this deep joy in our being because we have all that we are made for. All that we are called to.

—M. BASIL PENNINGTON

BENEDICT 480–547

Benedict of Nursia is considered the founder of Western monasticism. His rule, which outlined a comprehensive and judicious way for monks to live in community, spread through the West and is still in use today.

BENEDICT, detail

THE THEOTOKOS

"My soul magnifies the Lord,
and my spirit rejoices in God my Savior,
for he has looked with favor
on the lowliness of his servant.
Surely, from now on all generations
will call me blessed;
for the Mighty One has done great things for me,
and holy is his name.
His mercy is for those who fear him
from generation to generation."

—LUKE 1:46–51 NRSV

THE THEOTOKOS

Mary, universally regarded as the "Mother of God," Theotokos, is shown here with as much beauty, gentleness, dignity, and grandeur as can be imagined. This distinctive title reveals a profound, endearing truth not only about Mary, but also about each one of us. We are invited wholeheartedly into the very relationship that she had with her Son. We can become "God-bearers" and bring him to all those whom we encounter.

Mary's willing "yes" to God was made in complete freedom. Following her example, we can also say "yes," bringing new life into the world.

THE THEOTOKOS

Theotokos is the Greek title of the mother of Jesus used especially in the East. Its literal English translations include "God-bearer," "Birth-giver of God," and "the one who gives birth to God."

THE THEOTOKOS, detail

PERPETUA AND FELICITY

For I am convinced
that neither death, nor life,
nor angels, nor rulers,
nor things present, nor things to come,
nor powers,
nor height, nor depth,
nor anything else in all creation,
will be able to separate us
from the love of God
in Christ Jesus our Lord.

—ROMANS 8:38–39 NRSV

PERPETUA AND FELICITY

There is also light within, our desires and longings, our aspirations to rise above what is of this world, to discover the perfection of love and a happiness we can never lose. Such happiness, and the love that is its secret, elude us however much we may relish a foretaste of them in our present experience. . . . Our longing is, ultimately, for what we cannot now have. . . . Happiness, complete and unending, is for later, not now.

> *Restless hearts will ache no more*
> *when in possession of the absolute good.*

—CARDINAL BASIL HUME

PERPETUA AND FELICITY

The deaths of Perpetua, a noble woman, and her slave, Felicity, together with other newly baptized converts in the city of Carthage in 203, is recorded in *The Passion of Perpetua and Felicity*, one of the earliest historical accounts of Christian martyrdom.

PERPETUA AND FELICITY, detail

FRANCIS OF ASSISI

Start by doing what's necessary,
then do what's possible;
and suddenly you are doing the impossible.

—FRANCIS OF ASSISI

SAINT FRANCIS

FRANCIS OF ASSISI

Now, wherever we are,
and in every place,
and at every hour,
throughout each time of each day,
may all of us honestly and humbly believe,
holding in our hearts
to love, honor,
adore, serve,
praise, bless,
glorify, exalt,
magnify and give thanks
to the Most High and Eternal God,
Trinity and Unity,
Amen.

Benediction, Saint Francis
—JON M. SWEENEY

FRANCIS 1181–1226

Francis of Assisi, an Italian friar and preacher, is one of the most venerated religious figures in history. Having abandoned a life of wealth and privilege, Francis gathered around him a following of both men and women dedicated to spreading the gospel and serving the poor.

FRANCIS OF ASSISI, detail

 # THE TRINITY

See what love the Father has given us,
that we should be called
children of God;
and that is what we are.

—1 JOHN 3:1 NRSV

THE TRINITY

As we place ourselves in front of the icon in prayer, we come to experience a gentle invitation to participate in the intimate conversation that is taking place among the three divine angels and to join them around the table. The movement from the Father toward the Son and the movement of both Son and Spirit toward the Father become a movement in which the one who prays is lifted up and held secure. . . . We come to see with our inner eyes that all engagements in this world can bear fruit only when they take place within this divine circle . . . the house of perfect love.

—HENRI J. M. NOUWEN

THE TRINITY, detail

BASIL OF CAESAREA

"Love the Lord your God
with all your heart and
with all your soul and
with all your strength and
with all your mind"; and,
"Love your neighbor as yourself."

—LUKE 10:27 NIV

BASIL

We must try to
keep the mind in tranquility.

For just as the eye which constantly shifts its gaze, now turning to the right or to the left, now incessantly peering up and down, cannot see distinctly what lies before it, the sight must be fixed firmly on the object in view if one would make his vision of it clear. So too man's mind when distracted by his countless worldly cares cannot focus itself distinctly on the truth.

—BASIL OF CAESAREA

BASIL OF CAESAREA 329–379

Often called Basil the Great, this Greek monk and bishop was an influential theologian. Through both his preaching and his writing he successfully defended orthodox belief against the rising heresies of his time. He was known for his care of the poor, and his rule for monastic life is still the predominant basis for religious life in the Eastern Church.

BASIL, detail

GREGORY OF NAZIANZUS

Proclaim the message;
be persistent
whether the time is favorable or unfavorable;
convince, rebuke, and encourage,
with the utmost patience in teaching.

—2 TIMOTHY 4:2 NRSV

GREGORY OF NAZIANZUS 329–390

As bishop of Nazianzus, Gregory is widely considered one of the most eloquent preachers of the early church. Sometimes referred to as Gregory "the Theologian," he was also a monk and a poet.

GREGORY OF NAZIANZUS

The Shepherd

Think again, and even now, how
    the famous Shepherd—the One
who lays His life down for His sheep,
    came pressing sore to find
the solo agent straying, lost
    upon the mountain's rugged hills,
how He found that wanderer, and having
    found it, bore it firmly
on His shoulders and, having done so,
    schlepped it back
    to its blinking, live community.
Having set it right, He numbered it
    among the sheep who never strayed.
A figure then, a puzzle: He lit
    a candle—see, His very Flesh—and swept
    an unkempt house, cleansing
    all the world of contagion. He sought
    the precious coin whose Royal
Image was obscured by stain.
Listen. Ever—now—He calls together
    all His friends the angels
    upon the finding of that coin,
    and makes them all partakers in His joy.

—SCOTT CAIRNS

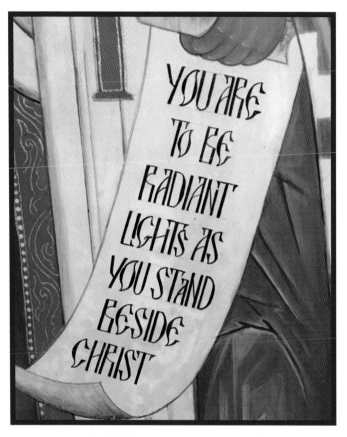

YOU ARE
TO BE
RADIANT
LIGHTS AS
YOU STAND
BESIDE
CHRIST

GREGORY OF NAZIANZUS, detail

GREGORY OF NYSSA

But, as it is written,
"What no eye has seen, nor ear heard,
nor the human heart conceived,
what God has prepared
for those who love him——"

—1 CORINTHIANS 2:9 NRSV

GREGORY OF NYSSA

Peace is defined as harmony
    among those who are divided.
When, therefore, we end the civil war
    within our nature and
    cultivate peace within ourselves,
    we become at peace.

—GREGORY OF NYSSA

GREGORY OF NYSSA 335–395

Together with his older brother Basil, and Gregory of Nazianzus, Gregory of Nyssa is known as one of the Cappadocian Fathers (for that region of present-day Turkey). A popular preacher, Gregory made significant contributions to supporting the theology of the Nicene Creed and the Trinity.

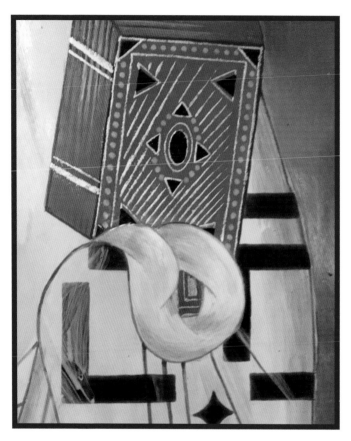

GREGORY OF NYSSA, detail

THE ANNUNCIATION

For with God nothing shall be impossible.
And Mary said, Behold the handmaid of the Lord;
be it unto me according to thy word.
And the angel departed from her.

—LUKE 1:37–38 KJV

THE ANNUNCIATION

Each day holds a surprise. But only if we expect it can we see, hear, or feel it when it comes to us. Let's not be afraid to receive each day's surprise, whether it comes to us as sorrow or as joy. It will open a new place in our hearts, a place where we can welcome new friends and celebrate more fully our shared humanity.

—HENRI J. M. NOUWEN

THE ANNUNCIATION, detail

JOHN CHRYSOSTOM

Finally, beloved, whatever is true,
whatever is honorable,
whatever is just, whatever is pure,
whatever is pleasing,
whatever is commendable, if there is any excellence
and if there is anything worthy of praise,
think about these things.

—PHILIPPIANS 4:8 NRSV

JOHN CHRYSOSTOM

Prayer is

the place of refuge for every worry,
a foundation for cheerfulness,
a source of constant happiness,
a protection against sadness.

—JOHN CHRYSOSTOM

JOHN CHRYSOSTOM 349–407

This major figure in Christian history is considered a "Doctor of the Church." After living the quiet life of a hermit he was ordained and appointed to the work of preaching, for which he was especially gifted, earning him the name of Chrysostom, meaning "golden-mouthed." He was made Patriarch of Constantinople in 398.

JOHN CHRYSOSTOM, detail

GREGORY THE GREAT

Therefore, since we are surrounded by such a great cloud of witnesses, let us throw off everything that hinders and the sin that so easily entangles, and let us run with perseverance the race marked out for us.

—HEBREWS 12:1 NIV

GREGORY THE GREAT

Have confidence in the compassion of our Creator. Reflect well on what you are now doing, and keep before you the things you have done. Lift up your eyes to the overflowing compassion of heaven, and while He waits for you, draw near in tears to our merciful Judge.

> *The God-Man gives man*
> *confidence before God.*
>
> —GREGORY THE GREAT

LET US STIR UP OUR FAITH AND FAN THE DESIRE FOR HEAVENLY THINGS

GREGORY THE GREAT, detail

THE NATIVITY

"Today in the town of David
a Savior has been born to you;
he is the Messiah, the Lord."

—LUKE 2:11 NIV

THE NATIVITY

This icon endears itself to the viewer, combining and gently illustrating all the stories around the birth of Christ. As we ponder the image in quiet we are comforted and encouraged by the many ways God orchestrated the lives of Mary and Joseph, the angels, the shepherds, and the wise men, drawing them to that special moment in time where God himself came down to earth as a small baby to save us. The image draws us into the wonder and sweetness of the moment, reassuring and challenging us to completely trust and worship along with heaven the child who would become our consolation and salvation.

THE NATIVITY, detail

JOHN THE BAPTIST

"And you, child,

   will be called the prophet of the Most High;
   for you will go before the Lord
   to prepare his ways,
   to give knowledge of salvation to his people
   by the forgiveness of their sins.
"By the tender mercy of our God,
   the dawn from on high
   will break upon us,
   to give light to those who sit in darkness
   and in the shadow of death,
   to guide our feet into the way of peace."

—LUKE 1:76–79 NIV

JOHN THE BAPTIST

Prayer is the place of refuge for every worry, a formulation for cheerfulness, a source of constant happiness, a protection against sadness.

—JOHN CHRYSOSTOM

. . . prayer is the sign of the great dignity with which the Creator has honored me. But at the same time it reminds me of my nothingness (I am of nothing, and have nothing of my own; therefore, I ask God for everything) and of my most high dignity (I am an image of God; I am made godly). . . .

—JOHN OF KRONSTADT

"He must increase,
but I must decrease."

—JOHN 3:30 NRSV

JOHN THE BAPTIST, detail

 **JOSEPH**

May the God of hope
fill you with all joy and peace
as you trust in him,
so that you may overflow
with hope
by the power of the Holy Spirit.

—ROMANS 15:13 NIV

JOSEPH

He was chosen by the eternal Father as the trustworthy guardian and protector of his greatest treasures, namely, his divine Son and Mary, Joseph's wife. He carried out this vocation with complete fidelity until at last God called him, saying: "Good and faithful servant, enter into the joy of your Lord."

—BERNARDINE OF SIENA

JOSEPH, detail

THE WASHING OF THE FEET

When he had finished washing their feet,
  he put on his clothes and returned to his place.
"Do you understand what I have done for you?"
  he asked them.
"You call me 'Teacher' and 'Lord,'
  and rightly so, for that is what I am.
Now that I, your Lord and Teacher,
  have washed your feet,
  you also should wash one another's feet.
I have set you an example that you should do
  as I have done for you.
Very truly I tell you, no servant is greater than his master,
  nor is a messenger greater
  than the one who sent him.
Now that you know these things,
  you will be blessed if you do them."
              —JOHN 13:12–17 NIV

THE WASHING OF THE FEET

Here in this icon there is a poignant sense of community. The icon shows Jesus's followers as completely defenseless and at a moment of greatest dependence on Him. It shows their intentions and desire to live together, their devotion to Jesus, and yet their obvious inability to stand as a group. It reveals their lack of strength to face danger and draw together in love.

There is a sweetness and benevolence about the figure of Christ, as if he understands our frailness and reaches out to our lostness and gathers about him our collective need. He is one of us in every sense. The disciples are almost happily scattered around the table, empathizing with each other, lost in their lack of understanding, hopeful for the future but completely misunderstanding the gravity of the moment. There is lovability in the shoes that are lost and the haphazardness of the poses. Like us, the disciples showed human fragility and weakness, but Jesus loved them dearly. Christ is the teacher, the humble conveyer of the love of God that passes all understanding, no matter what we might be going through.

THE WASHING OF THE FEET, detail

STEPHEN

But filled with the Holy Spirit, he gazed into heaven
and saw the glory of God and Jesus standing at the
right hand of God. "Look," he said,

> *"I see the heavens opened*
> *and the Son of Man standing*
> *at the right hand of God!"*

But they covered their ears, and with a loud shout
all rushed together against him. Then they dragged
him out of the city and began to stone him; and the
witnesses laid their coats at the feet of a young man
named Saul. While they were stoning Stephen, he
prayed, "Lord Jesus, receive my spirit." Then he knelt
down and cried out in a loud voice, "Lord, do not hold
this sin against them." When he had said this, he died.

—ACTS 7:55–60 NRSV

STEPHEN

Compassionate and forgiving Father, you give us grace to practice what we worship. Teach us to love our enemies as we keep the feast of your servant Stephen, who prayed even for those who stoned him to death. We ask this through our Lord Jesus Christ, your Son, who lives and reigns with you and the Holy Spirit, one God forever and ever. Amen.

—Collect from St. Stephen's Feast Day

STEPHEN, detail

 PHILIP

Philip said to him,
> *"Lord, show us the Father,*
> *and we will be satisfied."*
Jesus said to him,
> *"Have I been with you all this time, Philip,*
> *and you still do not know me?*
> *Whoever has seen me has seen the Father.*
> *How can you say, 'Show us the Father'?*
Do you not believe that I am in the Father
> *and the Father is in me?*
The words that I say to you
> *I do not speak on my own;*
> *but the Father who dwells in me does his works.*
Believe me that I am in the Father
> *and the Father is in me. . . ."*

—JOHN 14:8–11A NRSV

SAINT ΓΙΛΙΡ

LORD
SHOW
US THE
FATHER
AND WE
SHALL BE
SATISFIED

PHILIP

We shall see beauty face to face, not the beauty shining through things, but beauty in itself. We shall see it directly, not mediated by things; we shall see beauty, not beautiful things; we shall see without veils; we shall simply see.

—ERNESTO CARDENAL

PHILIP, detail

THE ANGEL BY THE TOMB

As they entered the tomb,
they saw a young man dressed in a
white robe sitting on the right side,
and they were alarmed.
"Don't be alarmed," he said.
"You are looking for Jesus
the Nazarene, who was crucified.

He has risen!
He is not here.

See the place where they laid him."

—LUKE 2:11 NIV

78

THE ANGEL BY THE TOMB

How many times have we gone to Christ hoping for an answer to our need and fears? Our Savior waits for us to run to him and gaze on his face. The perfect quality of this icon is that it so undoubtedly shows Jesus sympathetic to our lostness and our desire to know he is alive and there for us. This icon shows so deeply that God comprehends this depth of need in our lives.

The women run to the tomb in desperation seeking the Lord. An angel, one of the sympathetic heralds who reach out to humanity in our confusion and loss, waits there to reassure and direct us to our Lord. He reaches out to our lost hearts and invites us to find him again and put our trust in him. The poignant strength of this icon seeks to remind us of the depth of Christ's desire to save us.

THE ANGEL BY THE TOMB, detail

ARCHANGEL MICHAEL

He will cover you with his pinions,
and under his wings you will find refuge;
his faithfulness is a shield and buckler.
You will not fear the terror of the night,
or the arrow that flies by day,
or the pestilence that stalks in darkness,
or the destruction that wastes at noonday.
For he will command his angels concerning you
to guard you in all your ways.
On their hands they will bear you up,
so that you will not dash your foot against a stone.

—PSALM 91:4–6, 11–12 NRSV

ARCHANGEL MICHAEL

Holy Spirit
I depend on you for my inspiration
    the wind at my back
    the breath in my lungs
    the Spirit in my heart
Guide me now
    to pray even without inspiration
    to learn even without exhilaration
    to puzzle even without enthusiasm
So that I am ready for your future
    prepared to listen when you speak
    primed to puzzle over experiences
    I can't understand
    poised to leave when you tell me to go.
                     Amen.

—JACK LEVISON

ARCHANGEL MICHAEL, detail

MARY OF EGYPT

For I am convinced
that neither death, nor life,
nor angels, nor rulers,
nor things present, nor things to come,
nor powers,
nor height, nor depth,
nor anything else in all creation,
will be able to separate us
from the love of God
in Christ Jesus our Lord.

—ROMANS 8:38–39 NRSV

ST MARY
EGYPT

BLESSED
IS GOD
WHO GIVES
FOR THE
SALVATION
OF SINS

MARY OF EGYPT

God cannot join our soul until we have consented, just as the lover cannot be joined to his love, however much he loves her, while she still loves others. But God is joined to our soul the very moment the soul loves him. It is an automatic union. As soon as the soul stops loving creatures, it is suspended, not in the void, because there is no void, but in the bottomless abyss that is God. The soul is automatically embraced by God.

—Ernesto Cardenal

MARY OF EGYPT, FIFTH CENTURY

After years of dissolute living in Alexandria, Mary joined a group of pilgrims on their way to Jerusalem, where she experienced a profound conversion. She dedicated the rest of her life to asceticism and prayer in the desert. Her "Life," seen as a model of repentance since the sixth century, forms part of the liturgy of Orthodox Churches on the Fifth Sunday of Lent.

MARY OF EGYPT, detail

PENTECOST

When the day of Pentecost had come,
they were all together in one place.
And suddenly from heaven
there came a sound
like the rush of a violent wind,
and it filled the entire house
where they were sitting.
Divided tongues, as of fire,
appeared among them,
and a tongue rested on each of them.
All of them were filled with the Holy Spirit
and began to speak in other languages,
as the Spirit gave them ability.

—ACTS 2:1–4 NRSV

PENTECOST

We are in need of a new beginning in our society, a new Pentecost, a change in each one of us and a change in our society. . . . The Holy Spirit gave the apostles a greater understanding of their faith and enabled them to commit themselves to do something about it, and the necessary courage to do so. Those are the gifts we need in our day, a deepening of our faith, the commitment to Christ and his gospel, and the courage to witness.

—ERNESTO CARDENAL

PENTECOST, detail

 PAUL

Not that I have already obtained this
or have already reached the goal;
but I press on to make it my own,
because Christ Jesus has made me his own.
Beloved, I do not consider that I have made it my own;
but this one thing I do:
forgetting what lies behind
and straining forward to what lies ahead,
I press on toward the goal for the prize
of the heavenly call of God in Christ Jesus.

—Philippians 3:12–14 nrsv

PAUL

I thank you for the gift of physical vision, which enables me to enjoy the beauty of the natural world I am able to see and leads me to ponder the beauty of the supernatural world that I cannot. I thank you for the gift of spiritual vision, enabling us to see the world as your Son, who is the Light of the World, reveals it to us. I thank you for the gift of imaginative vision, encouraged and nourished in us by artists and writers, seers who seek, through their work, to reveal the spiritual truth and beauty they perceive. May I, like the blind man at Bethesda and like St. Paul, be touched by Christ this day and experience both the beginning of vision and the full clarity of sight offered by your word.

—ANGELA ALAIMO O'DONNELL

PAUL, detail

BARNABAS

Therefore, as God's chosen people,
holy and dearly loved,
clothe yourselves with compassion,
kindness, humility,
gentleness and patience.
Bear with each other
and forgive one another
if any of you has a grievance against someone.
Forgive as the Lord forgave you.

—COLOSSIANS 3:12–13 NIV

BARNABAS

Holy Spirit
  Come to me!
  Fill me!
  Inspire me!

No, that's not right
  Be the source of wisdom in my life
  Become the spring of discernment
        throughout my days
  Mature in me as the Spirit of God

Not while my hands are held high in worship
But while they are cuffed by hardship
  In drudgery and setbacks
  In delays and interruptions
  Interminable waiting

Yes, that's right, Holy Spirit.
  While life batters and bruises
  Be the source of wisdom
  Become the spring of discernment
  Mature in me as the Spirit of God
              Amen

—JACK LEVISON

BARNABAS, detail

THE TRANSFIGURATION

After six days Jesus took with him
  Peter, James and John the brother of James,
  and led them up a high mountain by themselves.
There he was transfigured before them.
His face shone like the sun, and his clothes
  became as white as the light.
Just then there appeared before them
  Moses and Elijah, talking with Jesus.
Peter said to Jesus, "Lord, it is good for us to be here.
If you wish, I will put up three shelters—one for you,
  one for Moses and one for Elijah."
While he was still speaking, a bright cloud covered them,
  and a voice from the cloud said,

> *"This is my Son,*
> *whom I love;*
> *with him I am well pleased.*
> *Listen to him!"*

—Matthew 17:1–5 niv

THE TRANSFIGURATION

If there is one icon that sums up the whole theology of icons, it is the Transfiguration. It shows that matter can be transformed by the power of God and can mediate God to us. The icon painter takes the most mundane materials—wood, minerals, lime oil—and by his God-given creative imagination, transforms them into a luminous image in God's praise.

—LINETTE MARTIN

THE TRANSFIGURATION, detail

Peter answered him,
>   *"Lord, if it is you,*
>   *command me to come to you on the water."*
He said, "Come."
So Peter got out of the boat,
>   *started walking on the water,*
>   *and came toward Jesus.*
But when he noticed the strong wind,
>   *he became frightened, and beginning to sink,*
>   *he cried out, "Lord, save me!"*
Jesus immediately reached out his hand
>   *and caught him, saying to him,*
"You of little faith, why did you doubt?"

—MATTHEW 14:28–31 NRSV

PETER

I think this experience you are having of losing your faith, or as you think, of having lost it, is an experience that in the long run belongs to faith.

. . . I don't know how the kind of faith required of a Christian . . . can be at all if it is not grounded on this experience . . . of unbelief. . . . Peter said, "Lord, I believe. Help my unbelief." It is the most natural and most agonizing prayer in the gospels, and I think it is the foundation prayer of faith.

—ANGELA ALAIMO O'DONNELL

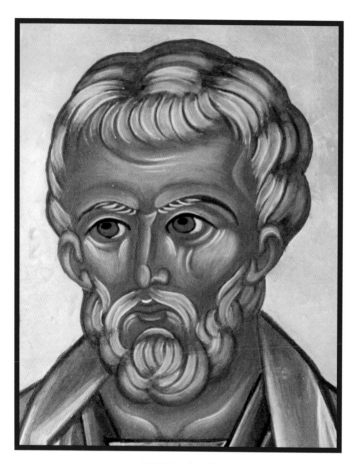

PETER, detail

IGNATIUS OF ANTIOCH

Through him you have
come to trust in God,
who raised him from the dead
and gave him glory,
so that your faith
and hope are set on God.

—1 PETER 1:21 NRSV

ST. IGNATIUS OF ANTIOCH

IGNATIUS OF ANTIOCH

Jesus wanted to show us his heart as the heart that loved so deeply.

God loved us,
he loved us with such great love.

The time for my birth [my entrance into heaven] is close at hand. Forgive me, my brothers. Do not stand in the way of my birth to real life; do not wish me stillborn. My desire is to belong to God. Do not, then, hand me back to the world. Do not try to tempt me with material things. Let me attain pure light. Only on my arrival there can I be fully a human being. Give me the privilege of imitating the passion of my God. If you have him in your heart, you will understand what I wish. You will sympathize with me because you will know what urges me on.

—IGNATIUS OF ANTIOCH

IGNATIUS OF ANTIOCH 35–108

Thought to have been a disciple of the apostle John, Ignatius is counted among the earliest of those church leaders and writers known as the "Apostolic Fathers." He is known particularly for the series of letters he wrote to Christians in the cities he passed on his way from Antioch to Rome, where tradition tells us he was martyred in the Colosseum.

IGNATIUS OF ANTIOCH, detail

Notes

4   Henri J. M. Nouwen, *The Inner Voice of Love*, Reprint Edition (New York: Image Books, 1999), 115.

12 M. Basil Pennington, *Listen with your Heart: Spiritual Living with the Rule of Saint Benedict* (Brewster, MA: Paraclete Press, 2007), 62.

20 Cardinal Basil Hume, *A Spiritual Companion: Reflections Through the Year* (Brewster, MA: Paraclete Press, 2001), 79.

24 Jon M. Sweeney, *The Saint Francis Prayer Book* (Brewster, MA: Paraclete Press, 2004), 125.

28 Henri J. M. Nouwen, *Behold the Beauty of the Lord: Praying with Icons*, Revised Edition (Notre Dame, IN: Ave Maria Press, 2007), 20–22.

36 Scott Cairns, *Love's Immensity: Mystics on the Endless Life* (Brewster, MA: Paraclete Press, 2007), 37-38.

44 Henri J. M. Nouwen, *Bread for the Journey: A Daybook of Wisdom and Faith*, Reprint Edition (San Francisco: HarperOne, 2006), 1.

76 Ernesto Cardenal, *Love, A Glimpse of Eternity* (Brewster, MA: Paraclete Press, 2006), 116.

84 Jack Levison, *40 Days with the Holy Spirit* (Brewster, MA: Paraclete Press, 2015), 37.

88 Ernesto Cardenal, *Love, A Glimpse of Eternity*, 68.

92 Ernesto Cardenal, *Love, A Glimpse of Eternity*, 29.

96 Angela Alaimo O'Donnell, *The Province of Joy: Praying with Flannery O'Conner* (Brewster, MA: Paraclete Press, 2012), 63–64.

100 Jack Levison, *40 Days with the Holy Spirit*, 49.

104 Linette Martin, *Sacred Doorways: A Beginners Guide to Icons* (Brewster, MA: Paraclete Press, 2002), 190.

108 Angela Alaimo O'Donnell, *The Province of Joy: Praying with Flannery O'Conner*, 121.

For Further Reading

Evseyeva, L. *A History of Icon Painting.* Moscow, Russia: Grand Holdings Publishers, 2005.

Lossky, Vladimir, and Leonid Ouspensky. *The Meaning of Icons.* 2nd edition. Yonkers, NY: St Vladimir's Seminary Press, 1999.

Martin, Linette. *Praying with Icons.* Brewster, MA: Paraclete Press, 2011.

———. *Sacred Doorways: A Beginner's Guide to Icons.* Brewster, MA: Paraclete Press, 2002.

Mathewes-Green, Frederica. *Welcome to the Orthodox Church: An Introduction to Eastern Christianity.* Brewster, MA: Paraclete Press, 2015.

Nes, Solrunn. *The Mystical Language of Icons.* Grand Rapids, MI: Eerdmans, 2009.

Nouwen, Henri J. M. *Behold the Beauty of the Lord: Praying with Icons.* Revised edition. Notre Dame, IN: Ave Maria Press, 2007.

———. *The Way of the Heart.* New York: Ballantine Books, 2003.

Rice, T. Talbot. *Icons Art and Devotion.* Publishers Overstock Remainder; 1st Edition in this form (November 1993).

Tradigo, Alfredo. *Icons and Saints of the Eastern Orthodox Church.* Los Angeles: J. Paul Getty Museum, 2006.

About Paraclete Press
WHO WE ARE

Paraclete Press is a publisher of books, recordings, and DVDs on Christian spirituality. Our publishing represents a full expression of Christian belief and practice—from Catholic to Evangelical, from Protestant to Orthodox.

We are the publishing arm of the Community of Jesus, an ecumenical monastic community in the Benedictine tradition. As such, we are uniquely positioned in the marketplace without connection to a large corporation and with informal relationships to many branches and denominations of faith.

WHAT WE ARE DOING

Paraclete Press Books | Paraclete publishes books that show the richness and depth of what it means to be Christian. Although Benedictine spirituality is at the heart of who we are and all that we do, we publish books that reflect the Christian experience across many cultures, time periods, and houses of worship. We publish books that nourish the vibrant life of the church and its people.

We have several different series, including the best-selling Paraclete Essentials and Paraclete Giants series of classic texts in contemporary English; Voices from the Monastery— men and women monastics writing about living a spiritual life today; our award-winning Paraclete Poetry series as well as the Mount Tabor Books on the arts; best-selling gift books for children on the occasions of baptism and first communion; and the Active Prayer Series that brings creativity and liveliness to any life of prayer.

Mount Tabor Books | Paraclete's newest series, Mount Tabor Books, focuses on the arts and literature as well as liturgical worship and spirituality, and was created in conjunction with the Mount Tabor Ecumenical Centre for Art and Spirituality in Barga, Italy.

Paraclete Recordings | From Gregorian chant to contemporary American choral works, our recordings celebrate the best of sacred choral music composed through the centuries that create a space for heaven and earth to intersect. Paraclete Recordings is the record label representing the internationally acclaimed choir Gloriæ Dei Cantores, praised for their "rapt and fathomless spiritual intensity" by *American Record Guide*; the Gloriæ Dei Cantores Schola, specializing in the study and performance of Gregorian chant; and the other instrumental artists of the Gloriæ Dei Artes Foundation.

Paraclete Press is also privileged to be the exclusive North American distributor of the recordings of the Monastic Choir of St. Peter's Abbey in Solesmes, France, long considered to be a leading authority on Gregorian chant.

Paraclete Videos | Our DVDs offer spiritual help, healing, and biblical guidance for a broad range of life issues including grief and loss, marriage, forgiveness, facing death, bullying, addictions, Alzheimer's, and spiritual formation.

Learn more about us at our website:
www.paracletepress.com
or phone us toll-free at 1.800.451.5006

SCAN
TO
READ
MORE

Also From Paraclete Press

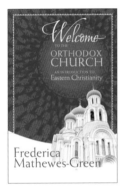

WELCOME TO THE ORTHODOX CHURCH
An Introduction to Eastern Christianity

Frederica Mathewes-Green

$19.99, Paperback | ISBN: 978-1-55725-921-9

"This excellent book is most valuable because it is more like a friend than a book. It's the voice you hope to hear beside you in church, murmuring explanations and encouragement as you make your journey. I highly recommend it."

—*Rev. Dr. Christopher Metropulos, Executive Director, Orthodox Christian Network*

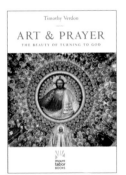

ART & PRAYER
The Beauty of Turning to God

Timothy Verdon

$34.99, Hardcover | ISBN: 978-1-61261-572-1

Renowned art historian Timothy Verdon explores how sacred art can teach us to pray in this stunningly beautiful, richly illustrated book. "Images put before believers can in fact teach them how to turn to God in prayer. . . . "

SACRED SONGS OF RUSSIA
Gloriæ Dei Cantores

$16.95, 70 min CD | ISBN: 978-1-55725-224-1

"This is the best—the best—compilation of standard Russian sacred choral music that I have ever heard . . ."
—*American Record Guide*